nature's
baby animals

BABY ANIMALS

OF THE MOUNTAINS

Carmen Bredeson

Dennis L. Claussen, PhD, *Series Science Consultant* Professor of Zoology, Miami University, Oxford, Ohio

Allan A. De Fina, PhD, *Series Literacy Consultant* Dean, College of Education/Department of Literacy Education, New Jersey City University, Jersey City, New Jersey; Past President of the NJ Reading Association

CONTENTS

WORDS TO KNOW

cliff (klif)—A high, steep rock on the side of a mountain.

enemy (EH nuh mee)—An animal that can hurt or kill another animal.

herd (hurd)—A group of animals that live together and eat plants.

MOUNTAINS

Mountains are very high places. Some mountains have snow on the top all year long. Other mountains are covered with rocks, trees, or grass. Baby animals have special ways to stay safe and live in the mountains.

BABY GIANT PANDA

A panda is pink when it is born.

A panda cub is the size of a banana when it is born. The cub's mother holds her baby close to keep it warm. Soon the cub's black and white hair grows. Then the little panda can stay warm in the cold mountain air.

Guanacos are good runners AND swimmers!

This baby can stand when it is born. Soon it is running with the **herd**. Guanacos [gwa NAH kohs] have thick pads on the bottoms of their feet. The pads help the guanacos walk on the rocky mountains.

BABY GUANACO

BABY MOUNTAIN LION

A mountain lion is also called a cougar or a puma.

Mountain lion cubs have black and brown spots on their fur. The fur blends into the rocks and grass. It is hard for an **enemy** to see the babies. When they are six months old, the cubs learn to hunt.

Baby mountain goats are born in the spring. Hours after they are born they can run and climb. Mountain goats are good jumpers. They jump from rock to rock. They can even jump straight UP!

BABY MOUNTAIN GOAT

Baby mountain goats are called kids.

BABY MOUNTAIN GORILLA

This baby holds tight to its mother's fur. She carries the baby while she looks for fruit and plants to eat. Gorillas are shy animals. They live in thick forests on the mountains.

A baby rock hyrax [HY raks] can run soon after it is born. It has feet that grip the rocks. When danger is near, the little hyrax runs up the mountain. It goes into a hiding place in the rocks.

BABY

ROCK HYRAX

BABY **PEREGRINE FALCON**

Peregrine [PAIR ih grin] falcon chicks are born on a **cliff**. They stay safe in their sky-high home. The chicks flap their wings to make them strong. Soon they will fly off the mountain.

Baby snow leopards grow thick fur. Their big, furry feet make walking in the mountain snow easier. Snow leopards have thick fur on their tails too. They curl up under the furry tails when they sleep.

BABY SNOW LEOPARD

Books

Dunphy, Madeleine. *The Peregrine's Journey*. Berkeley, Calif.: Web of Life Children's Books, 2008.

Gordon, Sharon. *Mountain Animals*. New York: Benchmark Books, 2008.

Macken, JoAnn Early. *Mountain Goats*. Strongsville, Ohio: Gareth Stevens Publishing, 2006.

Ostby, Kristin. *A Baby Panda is Born*. New York: Grosset & Dunlap, 2008.

Schreiber, Anne. *Pandas.* Washington, D.C.: National Geographic Children's Books, 2010.

National Geographic
http://kids.nationalgeographic.com/Animals/
CreatureFeature/Mountain-gorilla

Watch a gorilla video. Hear gorilla sounds.

San Diego Zoo
http://www.sandiegozoo.org/pandacam/index.html

Watch a live panda camera.

INDEX

~For Kate and Caroline, our beautiful granddaughters~

Enslow Elementary, an imprint of Enslow Publishers, Inc.
Enslow Elementary® is a registered trademark of Enslow Publishers, Inc.

Copyright © 2011 by Carmen Bredeson

Library of Congress Cataloging-in-Publication Data

Bredeson, Carmen.
  Baby animals of the mountains / Carmen Bredeson.
    p. cm. — (Nature's baby animals)
  Includes bibliographical references and index.
  Summary: "Up-close photos and information about baby animals of the mountains"—
Provided by publisher.
  Library Ed. ISBN 978-0-7660-3562-1
  Paperback ISBN 978-1-59845-225-9
  1. Mountain animals—Infancy—Juvenile literature. I. Title.
  QL113.B65 2011
  591.753—dc22

                    2009037898

Printed in the United States of America
102010 Lake Book Manufacturing, Inc., Melrose Park, IL

10 9 8 7 6 5 4 3 2 1

♻ Enslow Publishers, Inc., is committed to printing our books on recycled paper. The paper
in every book contains 10% to 30% post-consumer waste (PCW). The cover board on the
outside of each book contains 100% PCW. Our goal is to do our part to help young people and
the environment too!

Every effort has been made to locate all copyright holders of material used in this book. If any
errors or omissions have occurred, corrections will be made in future editions of this book.

Photo Credits: © Art Wolfe/Getty Images, p. 13; © Daniel Cox/Photolibrary.com, p. 11;
© Daniel J. Cox/NaturalExposures.com, p. 20; © Katherine Feng/Minden Pictures, p. 7;
© Kemp Richard & Julia/Photolibrary.com, p. 19; © Lisa & Mike Husar/TeamHusar.com,
pp. 1, 6, 23; © NHPA/Photoshot, pp. 2 (right), 18; © Peter Arnold, Inc./Alamy, p. 10;
© Peter Lilja/Getty Images, p. 9; © Rose, A./Peter Arnold Inc., p. 21; Shutterstock, p. 5;
© Smith, Charles R/Animals Animals, p. 12; © Thomas Marent/Visuals Unlimited, Inc., p. 15;
© WILDLIFE/Peter Arnold Inc., pp. 2 (left), 14, 16, 17; © Yva Momatiuk & John Eastcott/
Minden Pictures, p. 8; Shutterstock, p. 3

Cover Photo: © Lisa & Mike Husar/TeamHusar.com

Note to Parents and Teachers: The *Nature's Baby Animals* series supports the National
Science Education Standards for K–4 science. The Words to Know section introduces subject-
specific vocabulary words, including pronunciation and definitions. Early readers may need
help with these new words.

Enslow Elementary
an imprint of
E | **Enslow Publishers, Inc.**
40 Industrial Road
Box 398
Berkeley Heights, NJ 07922
USA
http://www.enslow.com